FACTIVITY

BLAST OFF

ON A MISSION

TO EXPLORE

SPACE

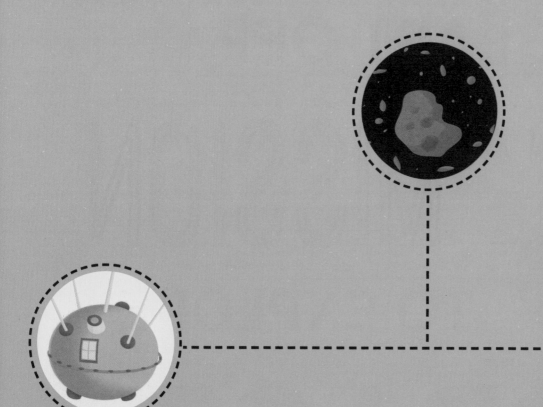

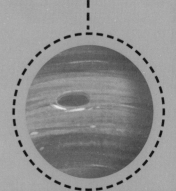

This edition published by Parragon Books Ltd in 2016 and distributed by

Parragon Inc.
440 Park Avenue South, 13th Floor
New York, NY 10016
www.parragon.com
Please retain this information for future reference.

Copyright © Parragon Books Ltd 2016

©2016 Discovery Communications, LLC. Discovery Kids and the
Discovery Kids logo are trademarks of Discovery Communications,
LLC, used under license. All rights reserved. discoverykids.com

Written by Tom Jackson
Illustrated by Mattia Cerato
Consultant: Peter Bond, FRAS, Fellow of the British Interplanetary Society

All rights reserved. No part of this publication may be reproduced, stored in a retrieval
system or transmitted, in any form or by any means, electronic, mechanical, photocopying,
recording or otherwise, without the prior permission of the copyright holder.

ISBN 978-1-4748-2040-0

Printed in China

Discovery KIDS™

BLAST OFF

ON A MISSION

TO EXPLORE

SPACE

PaRRagon

Bath • New York • Cologne • Melbourne • Delhi
Hong Kong • Shenzhen • Singapore

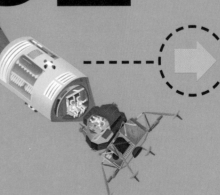

Contents

Here we go...
Blast off into amazing
outer space!

You'll find activity answers at the back of the book.

Flip to the glossary for special space words.

Welcome to space

Have you ever looked up at night at the darkness and the stars? You are looking into outer space! Space looks black because most of it is empty.

GALAXY

STARS

Most of the lights in the night sky are **stars**. They are like our Sun, but look less bright because they are much farther away from us.

Some of the lights in the sky don't come from stars. Some are **galaxies**: huge groups of stars packed together.

Stars are much too far away to visit! But scientists can study them using super-powerful telescopes.

People who study the things in space are called astronomers.

NEBULA

Other lights in the sky are from clouds of glowing **gas**, called **nebulas**.

MOON

The nearest thing to us in space is the Moon. It looks big because it is so close to Earth. But actually, the Moon is more than a million times SMALLER than a star.

PLANETS

Some lights in the sky move around differently to the stars. Some of these are **planets**.

About 500 people have traveled into space so far. Inventions such as rockets and spacesuits have made this possible!

Where is space!

The distance from Earth's surface to space is 60 miles. To get there you just go straight up! Between the ground and outer space is a layer of air called the **atmosphere**.

... so I need a spacesuit to help me breathe!

The air is so thin that no airplane can fly here. Only rockets and spacecraft go higher than this!

THERMOSPHERE

Tiny traces of air spread more than 400 miles into space. Spacecraft **orbiting** Earth fly through this very thin layer of atmosphere.

Tiny fast-moving particles from the Sun make the atmosphere glow up here. The light is called the **aurora**

MESOSPHERE

The air is very thin here. Specks of dust from space burn up as they hit the mesosphere, making streaks of light—a **meteor** shower!

400 MILES

60 MILES—SPACE

UP TO 45 MILES

unlike a jet engine. So rockets can fly in space.

The highest-flying aircraft only travel about a quarter of the way to space. From this height pilots can see the curve of the Earth.

Passenger jets fly at the top of the troposphere. It's as cold as the South Pole up here. Brr!

I need to wear a special protective suit to stay alive here!

At about 30,000 feet tall, Mount Everest is the highest place on Earth.

The air is so thin up here that I have to breathe air from a tank!

UP TO 30 MILES

STRATOSPHERE

This layer contains a gas called **ozone**. The gas blocks dangerous rays from space so they don't reach us down on the ground.

UP TO 12 MILES

TROPOSPHERE

The lower layer contains most of the air. This is where all our weather happens.

What's in space?

Earth is surrounded by space. We call it space because most of it is, well... empty space! But, among all that emptiness, there are many things to see.

Universe
The whole of space together is called the **universe**. There is only one universe and you can see it in whichever direction you look.

The universe is still growing and gets bigger every day.

Galaxy
Stars in the universe are grouped together in huge clusters called galaxies. The universe has about 100 billion galaxies—that's 12 galaxies for every person on Earth!

Nebulas are clouds of gas and dust out in space. They are where stars are born. Many nebulas are named after their shapes. Match the name to the nebula!

❶ Butterfly nebula

❷ Cat's eye nebula

❸ Horsehead nebula

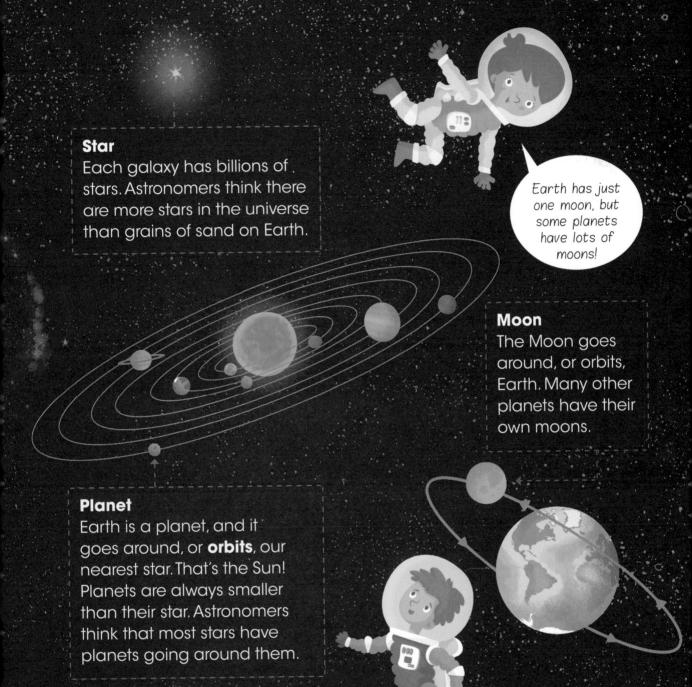

Star

Each galaxy has billions of stars. Astronomers think there are more stars in the universe than grains of sand on Earth.

Earth has just one moon, but some planets have lots of moons!

Moon

The Moon goes around, or orbits, Earth. Many other planets have their own moons.

Planet

Earth is a planet, and it goes around, or **orbits**, our nearest star. That's the Sun! Planets are always smaller than their star. Astronomers think that most stars have planets going around them.

B

C

Speed of light

The universe is enormous and everything in it is really spread out. It's too big to measure in feet and miles—the distances are too huge to write down!

Instead of using miles, astronomers measure the universe in light-years.

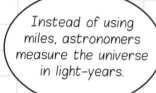

One light-year is the distance a beam of light travels in one year.

The nearest star is 28,800,000,000,000 miles away—or 4 light-years. That's much easier to write down!

The next time there's a thunderstorm, you can find out how fast light travels compared to sound.

You will need:
- A stopwatch
- Notepaper
- A calculator

1 Set yourself up safely inside and watch for lightning from a window.

KABOOM!

2 As soon as you see a flash, press start on the stopwatch. You could also just count out loud, clearly and slowly, like this: 1 second, 2 seconds, 3 seconds…

3 Stop counting when you hear the thunder. How many seconds did you count? Write the number down.

That tells you how far away the thunder and lightning were. So if it took 15 seconds to hear the sound, the lightning was 3 miles away!

_____ seconds

÷

5

= _____ miles

4 Divide the number of seconds between the lightning flash and the thunderclap by five.

The light and sound come from the same place, but the light is so fast it gets to you much, much sooner. You have to wait for the sound to catch up!

Gravity

To understand space, you need to know about the invisible force that holds it all together: **gravity**. Everything in the universe produces a force of gravity that pulls on everything else—even you!

To get into space, we have to overcome the pull of gravity.

Gravity gives things weight. Your weight is a measure of how much Earth is pulling on your body.

Skydivers fall because they are pulled by Earth's gravity. Gravity pulls everything on Earth toward the center of the planet and stops us from floating off into space!

Heavier objects have a more powerful pull of gravity than lighter ones. The Sun's gravity is 28 times stronger than the gravity on Earth.

An open parachute catches the air and slows down skydivers to a safe speed to land.

The force of gravity gets weaker and weaker as you move away from an object, so the Earth has a bigger pull on us than the Sun.

Why? Earth's gravity is pulling on all of the objects, so they all fall the same!

Check the object that you think has the most gravity.

☐ Tennis ball   ☐ Ping-pong ball
☐ Rock   ☐ Basketball

Now test your guesses!

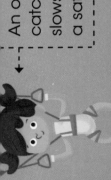

JUNIOR ASTRONOMER!

You will need:
- A basketball
- A tennis ball
- A ping-pong ball
- A rock

1 Drop two of the objects at the exact same time from the exact same level. Which one hits the ground first?

2 Now drop the other two. What happens? Swap the objects around and drop them again.

3 What are you finding? You should see that the big objects fall in the same way as the small ones, and they all hit the ground at the same time!

15

The Big Bang!

The universe is 13.8 billion (13,800,000,000) years old. In all that time space has just kept on getting bigger and bigger. But where exactly did it all come from?

① TIME BEGINS

To begin with, everything that makes up the universe was packed inside a tiny dot of space. It was very hot and began to **expand**… in a **Big Bang!**

② 3 MINUTES

Soon, the whole of space filled with light and other rays.

 Make your own expanding universe! As space expands, or gets bigger, everything in it spreads out. You can see how this happens by blowing up a balloon.

① Draw galaxies on a deflated balloon with a marker pen.

② Ask an adult to help you blow up the balloon.

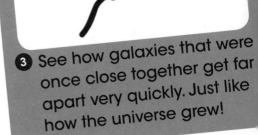

③ See how galaxies that were once close together get far apart very quickly. Just like how the universe grew!

Warning! Children can choke or suffocate on uninflated or broken balloons. Adult supervision required. Keep uninflated balloons away from children and discard broken balloons at once.

❸ 300,000 YEARS

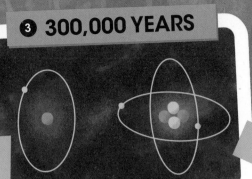

As the universe got bigger, it began to cool down. **Atoms** of **hydrogen** and helium started to form.

❹ 1 BILLION YEARS

The atoms formed into huge clouds of gas that were pulled together by gravity, making the very first stars and galaxies.

❺ 13 BILLION YEARS

Over billions of years, atoms made by the first stars were used to make new stars and planets. This is where we are now!

Atoms are the building blocks that make up everything in the universe—stars, planets, and you, too!

The Milky Way

Our planet Earth, the Sun, and almost all the stars in the night sky are part of a galaxy called the Milky Way. You could call the Milky Way our "home town" in space.

On dark nights you can see a pale band that runs through the middle of the sky. We call this the Milky Way.

The Milky Way is actually a huge swirling spiral of stars. It contains between 100 billion and 200 billion stars. That's at least 14 stars for every person living on Earth!

The Milky Way was made from other galaxies coming together.

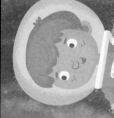

We call our galaxy the Milky Way because it looks like milk spilt across the sky!

YOU ARE HERE!

The Sun and Earth are halfway from the center of the Milky Way. The whole galaxy is spinning in space and it takes Earth 225 million years to go around just once!

There are lots of amazing galaxies in the universe. Match the galaxy to its name.

1 Whirlpool Galaxy   **2** Tadpole Galaxy   **3** Milky Way (from our viewpoint)

C

B

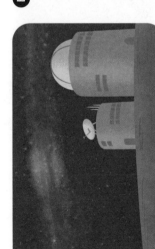

A

The Solar System

Our **Solar System** is made up of the Sun, Earth, seven other planets, and all the other objects that travel around the Sun.

Sun
The Sun is the hot star at the center of the Solar System. The planets move around the Sun in oval paths called orbits.

Venus
Size: 0.95 Earths
Moons: 0

Mercury
Size: 0.4 Earths
Moons: 0

Mars
Size: 0.5 Earths
Moons: 2

Earth
Moons: 1

Jupiter
Size: 11 Earths
Moons: 67

Uranus
Size: 4 Earths
Moons: 27

JUNIOR ASTRONOMER!

You will need:
- Toilet paper
- Coloring pens

Want to get an idea of how far apart the planets in our Solar System are? Build a toilet paper version to see for yourself!

1 Start by making a dot ½ inch wide on the first sheet of paper. This is the Sun

Asteroid Belt

Between Mars and Jupiter there's a ring of space rocks called the Asteroid Belt. There are millions of rocks, ranging in size from a few yards wide to a rock as big as France!

Saturn

Size: 9.5 Earths
Moons: 62

Ice belt

Around the outside of the Solar System is a cloud made of chunks of ice. Pluto is one of the biggest objects in this area.

Neptune

Size: 3.9 Earths
Moons: 14

Planets spin as they orbit the Sun. Our day is the time it takes for Earth to spin around once.

Sometimes the ice chunks fly toward the Sun and become comets!

Unroll the paper and make a dot for Mercury on the fourth sheet along.

❸ Make dots for the other planets:

7th sheet: Venus
10th sheet: Earth
15th sheet: Mars
52nd sheet: Jupiter
95th sheet: Saturn
191st sheet: Uranus
300th sheet: Neptune

There should be enough toilet paper in a single roll. You will need 110 feet to roll out your whole Solar System!

The Sun

The Sun gives our planet light and heat. It is 93 million miles away but its rays take just eight minutes to reach us.

Corona
The Sun is surrounded by a wispy layer of hot gas. This is called the corona. It is actually the hottest part of the Sun!

Luckily the Sun is very far away, so things on Earth don't melt!

Temperature
The Sun's surface is 10,000°F. That is hot enough to melt everything on Earth!

Solar flare
Huge clouds of hot gas called solar flares blast out of the Sun's surface.

Surface
The surface of the Sun is not solid. It is made up of superheated glowing gases called plasma.

Size
The Sun is very big. It is 100 times wider than Earth. More than a million Earths could fit inside it!

Sunspot
Cooler patches on the surface appear as dark "sunspots."

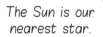

The Sun is our nearest star.

JUNIOR ASTRONOMER!

You can tell the time from the position of shadows made by the Sun. Make a sundial to see this for yourself! Build your sundial in the morning so that you can read it at 12 noon.

You will need:

- A drinking straw
- A paper plate
- Pens
- A clock

1. Copy the numbers from a clock onto the paper plate, with 12 at the top.

2. Ask an adult to cut a hole in the middle of the plate and push the straw through so it stands up straight.

3. At midday, take the sundial to a sunny place and turn it around until the shadow of the straw points at the 12. Now you're ready to tell time!

4. The shadow moves as the Sun's position in the sky changes. The shadow will point to the right time until sunset.

To us, it looks like the Sun moves across the sky. But, it actually stays still and it's us that's moving as Earth spins around.

23

Earth

Earth is our home in space. It is a very special planet. It is the only place in the universe where we know that life exists. That life includes you!

Axis
Like all the planets, Earth is rotating a bit like a toy top. It spins around a line called the **axis**, which runs through the North and South Poles.

Earth's axis tilts over to one side!

Equator
The equator is an invisible line that runs around the middle of Earth (or any planet). The top half of the planet is called the Northern Hemisphere. The bottom half is the Southern Hemisphere.

Continents
Earth's surface is a layer of rocks called the crust. The thicker bits of crust stick out of the ocean to form dry land.

Force field

At its center, Earth has a large metal core that works like a giant **magnet** and sends out a force field into space. This protects Earth from high-energy particles that come from the Sun (the solar wind).

Earth takes one year to orbit the Sun, and has four seasons in that time: winter, spring, summer, and fall. These are caused by the tilt of Earth's axis and how high this makes the Sun appear in the sky.

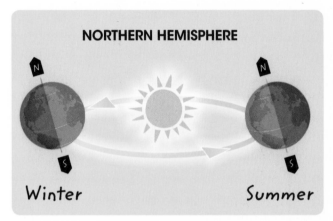

NORTHERN HEMISPHERE

Winter   Summer

Label the seasons for the Southern Hemisphere.

1 [ ]   2 [ ]

SOUTHERN HEMISPHERE

Oceans

Earth is the only place in the Solar System to have oceans of water on its surface. Everywhere else is either too hot, so the water boils away, or too cold, so it freezes into ice.

Here's a hint… In the Southern Hemisphere, the seasons are the opposite!

The Moon

Earth has just one moon. It is the closest neighbor we have in space. It orbits around us as Earth orbits around our Sun—so wherever Earth is in space, the Moon is too!

No one is sure where the Moon came from. The best guess is that another planet hit Earth and the explosion blasted a lot of rocks into space. These all clumped together to make our moon.

From Earth, you can see lots of dark patches on the Moon's surface. Ancient astronomers thought they were patches of water. They gave them names like Sea of Tranquility, Ocean of Storms, and Bay of Rainbows. But actually, there is no liquid water on the Moon at all!

We still use those names today!

TALLEST MOUNTAIN

The Moon has its own mountain ranges. The tallest mountain is near the South Pole and is about 7,000 feet taller than Mount Everest on Earth!

The Moon is a quarter of the size of Earth. That makes it a very large moon indeed. No other planet in our Solar System has a moon that is so close to its size.

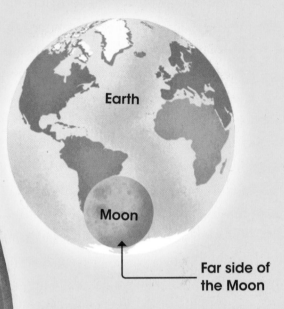

Earth

Moon

Far side of the Moon

We can only see one side of the Moon from Earth, but spacecraft have visited the hidden far side.

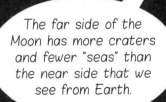

The far side of the Moon has more craters and fewer "seas" than the near side that we see from Earth.

Craters galore!

The Moon is covered in millions of craters. These were formed when rocks called **meteorites** hit the Moon and left big holes. Some craters are as big as a city!

Rim
The rim rises up around the outside of the crater like a ring-shaped hill. It forms from all the rock thrown out of the crater when the meteorite hit.

Meteor
There are tiny meteorites hitting the Moon every day.

The largest crater on the Moon, called the Aitken basin, is 1,500 miles wide. That's the distance between New York City and Houston, Texas!

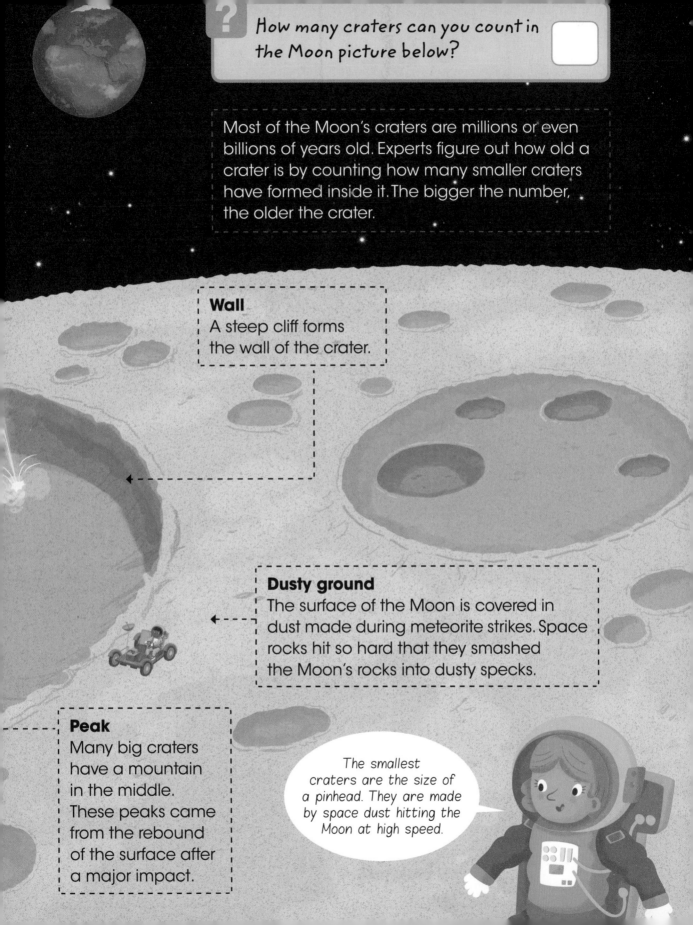

How many craters can you count in the Moon picture below?

Most of the Moon's craters are millions or even billions of years old. Experts figure out how old a crater is by counting how many smaller craters have formed inside it. The bigger the number, the older the crater.

Wall
A steep cliff forms the wall of the crater.

Dusty ground
The surface of the Moon is covered in dust made during meteorite strikes. Space rocks hit so hard that they smashed the Moon's rocks into dusty specks.

Peak
Many big craters have a mountain in the middle. These peaks came from the rebound of the surface after a major impact.

The smallest craters are the size of a pinhead. They are made by space dust hitting the Moon at high speed.

Just a phase

The Moon doesn't make light of its own like the Sun. We can see it because it reflects the Sun's light like a giant mirror. Depending on where it is in relation to the Sun, the Moon has a different shape in the sky. These shapes are known as its **phases**.

 Color the dotted areas black to reveal the phases of the Moon.

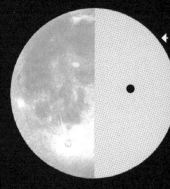

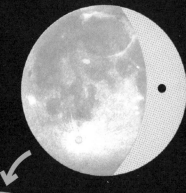

Full Moon
The Moon appears as a round disk in the sky. Earth is between the Sun and the Moon, so we can see all of the Moon's lit surface.

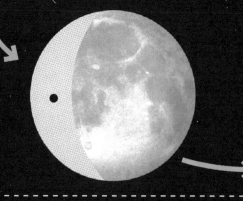

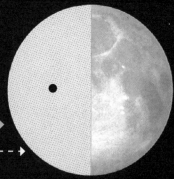

Half Moon, waning side
After the Full Moon, the Moon appears to "shrink" again, into another Half Moon.

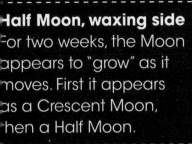

Half Moon, waxing side

For two weeks, the Moon appears to "grow" as it moves. First it appears as a Crescent Moon, then a Half Moon.

Over a month, a Full Moon shrinks then grows back to a Full Moon.

LUNAR MONTH

Then it starts all over again!

It takes a week for the New Moon to become a Half Moon.

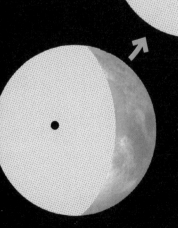

New Moon

The Moon is between Earth and the Sun. The Moon's lit surface is facing away from us, so we cannot see anything.

In the shadows

Imagine if the Sun just disappeared in the middle of the day! All of a sudden, it would go as dark as night. This happens during a special event called a solar eclipse.

It's not safe to look directly at the Sun, so people wear special glasses to watch a solar eclipse.

SOLAR ECLIPSE

The shadow of the Moon covers a small patch of Earth and the shadow moves quickly across the Earth's surface. When you're in the shadow, you'll see the Sun gradually covered by a black area and then just disappear. You can still see the hot gas, or corona, that surrounds the Sun, glowing around the shadow.

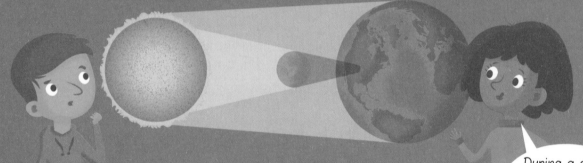

During a solar eclipse, the Sun is blocked out by the Moon.

LUNAR ECLIPSE

We can also see lunar eclipses, where the Moon disappears. During a lunar eclipse the Earth's shadow covers a Full Moon. The Moon often turns an orange color, and it's safe to look at without eye protection.

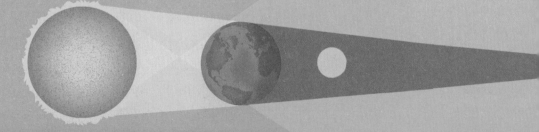

JUNIOR ASTRONOMER!

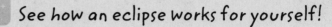

You will need:

- Fruit to represent the Moon, such as a round cherry
- Fruit to represent the Earth, such as a round melon
- A dark room
- A flashlight or cell phone flashlight app to represent the Sun
- A wooden skewer

1 Place the cherry "Moon" on the skewer.

2 Place the melon "Earth" on a flat surface and the flashlight "Sun" 11 inches away.

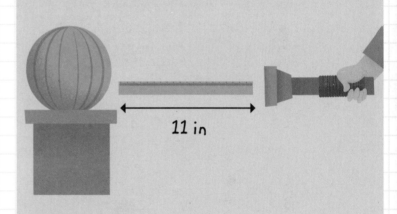

11 in

3 Using the skewer, hold the "Moon" between the "Earth" and "Sun".

What do you see on the "Earth's" surface?

Rocky planets

The first four planets in the Solar System are made of rocks and metals. Metal forms the core of the planet, while rock forms a hard outer crust.

Mercury
Mercury is hard to see in the sky and never stays in the same place for long. Living on Mercury would be very strange. From sunrise to sunset, a day on Mercury lasts the same amount of time as 176 days on Earth!

Venus
Venus is the hottest planet in the Solar System. Its surface is 850°F—much hotter than an oven! It rains acid on Venus, and the air is so thick and heavy it would squash a human body. It has a thick cloud layer, so we can't actually see its surface.

Eek, get me out of here!

Venus is the brightest planet in the sky and was named after the Roman goddess of love.

Sun

Mars
Mars looks red because it is covered in rocks and sand made of iron **minerals**, which have turned a rusty color.

The same sort of iron minerals make your blood look red, too!

Mars was the Roman god of war.

Mars has two little moons called Phobos and Deimos. It is thought these were space rocks from far away that flew very close to Mars and got trapped by its gravity.

Earth
Huge rocky chunks are moving around on Earth's surface. They move just a few inches a year, but over many millions of years the shape of the land and oceans changes completely.

True or false?

		TRUE	FALSE
❶	On Mercury it is dark all the time. The Sun never comes up.	☐	☐
❷	Venus is the hottest planet in the Solar System.	☐	☐
❸	Earth's land is always moving—just very slowly.	☐	☐
❹	Mars is red because its surface is covered in seaweed.	☐	☐

Venus and Mars

Mars and Venus are Earth's nearest neighbors. For centuries people thought that these planets might be a lot like Earth. But then space probes showed they are very strange, different worlds.

VENUS FACT FILE

After the Sun and Moon, Venus is the brightest object in our sky. It has a thick, cloudy atmosphere that reflects much of the Sun's light.

It is impossible to see through Venus's cloudy atmosphere. No one knew what its surface looked like until the Magellan space probe made a map using radar waves.

The map showed that, 500 million years ago, the whole of Venus's surface erupted like a volcano and covered the entire planet in lava!

MARS FACT FILE

Mars has volcanoes and huge rocky canyons just like Earth does. But they are much, much bigger!

Mars has a canyon called Valles Marineris. It is 11 times longer than the Grand Canyon and four times deeper. If the canyon was on Earth, it would stretch all the way across the United States!

The largest mountain on Mars is a volcano called Olympus Mons. It is also the tallest mountain in the entire Solar System and is more than twice as high as Mount Everest.

JUNIOR ASTRONOMER!

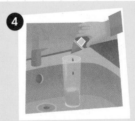

Get a grown-up to help you make your very own Martian volcano!

You will need:

- A tall, narrow glass
- Baking soda
- Food dye (different colors)
- Vinegar

Martian means "from Mars"!

1  Put the glass in a sink (this could get messy!). Add a spoonful of baking soda.

2  Add two drops of food dye. Be careful—food dye can stain!

3  Stir, and then add another spoonful of baking soda and a different color of dye.

4 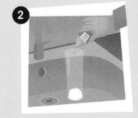 Do this a few more times.

5 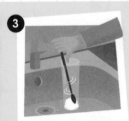 Now pour in enough vinegar to cover the powder.

6  Stand well back and watch. Colorful lava will erupt from your volcano!

The Asteroid Belt

Between the four rocky planets and four outer planets in the Solar System there is a ring of rocks called the Asteroid Belt.

Asteroids are made from rocks and metals. Astronomers think they are leftovers from when our Solar System was formed billions of years ago.

In 2001, a spacecraft called NEAR become the only man-made object ever to land on an asteroid.

Help the Cassini probe navigate through the Asteroid Belt to Jupiter.

START

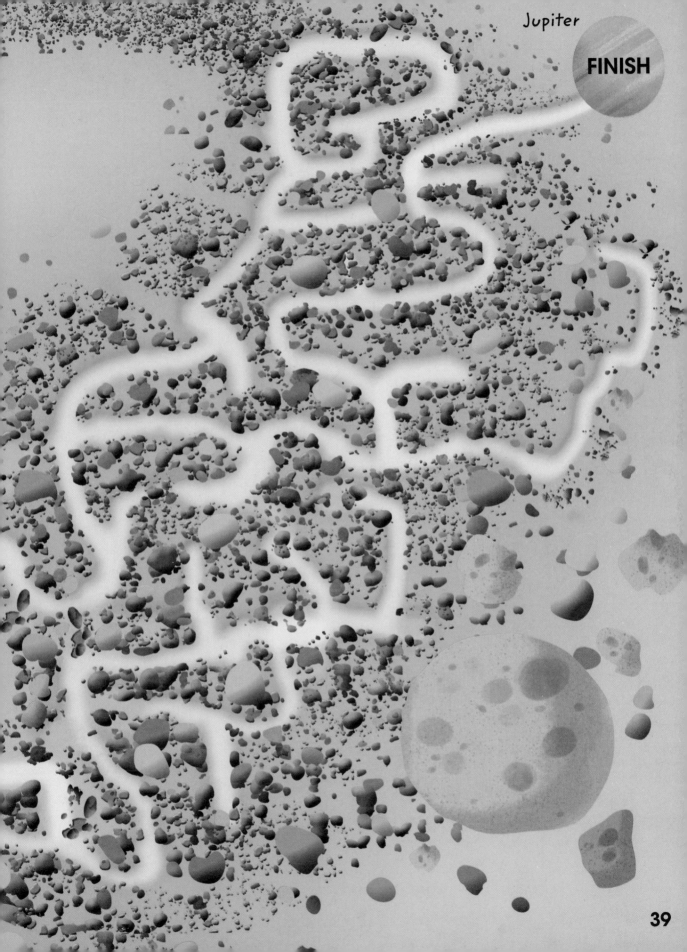

Jupiter

FINISH

Jupiter

Jupiter is the largest planet in the Solar System. It weighs more than all the other planets put together!

Jupiter is a kind of planet called a **gas giant**. Almost all the planet is made up of thick, swirling layers of gas and liquid (hydrogen and helium).

Jupiter spins very fast. Even though it is 12 times wider than Earth, it spins around in less than 10 hours!

No one knows for sure, but deep inside Jupiter there is probably a solid core of rock and ice about the same size as Earth.

Jupiter is a very windy place. The clouds whizz along at 250 mph.

That's about as fast as a tornado's wind on Earth.

Can you spot five differences in the bottom picture of Jupiter?

Because the planet spins so fast, its clouds spread out into bands. Some bands move faster than others, so Jupiter is always changing the way it looks.

The Great Red Spot is more than twice as wide as Earth!

Jupiter's clouds are full of storms. The biggest is the Great Red Spot. This storm has been raging for more than 300 years. No one knows why it's so long or so red!

Saturn

Saturn is the second largest planet in our Solar System. It is another gas giant, like Jupiter. It is most famous for its amazing rings.

Close up
From far away, Saturn's rings look solid. However, up close you can see that they are actually made of billions of tiny lumps of rock and ice.

Saturn's rings probably formed when a large moon got smashed to bits and all the pieces spread out.

Size
The rings all together are very wide—more than double the width of Saturn. They are also very thin. In most places they are less than 300 feet thick.

Color the rings with a dot using a bright color. The dark rings between them are areas where there are fewer tiny particles.

Shepherd moon
Larger rocks known as **shepherd moons** orbit inside the rings. They stop the ring particles from spreading out.

Weight
Saturn is almost as big as Jupiter but weighs only a third as much.

Uranus

The two outer planets in the Solar System are Uranus and Neptune. They are both about four times wider than Earth, and they are made up of mostly ices.

Rings
Uranus and Neptune have rings like Saturn, but they can only be seen with the biggest telescopes.

Uranus
Uranus was named after the ancient Greek god of the sky, who was the father of Saturn.

Earth

Uranus

Tilt
All the other planets rotate like a toy top as they orbit the Sun. Uranus spins on its side.

Because of the tilt of Uranus, each pole stays in sunlight for 21 years, while the opposite pole stays in complete darkness.

Neptune

Neptune
Neptune is a deep blue color. Because of this color, astronomers named it after Neptune, the god of the sea.

Actually, there is no liquid water on Neptune at all!

With wind speeds of up to 1,200 mph, Neptune has the strongest winds in the Solar System.

Like Jupiter, Neptune has storms that we can see. In 1989, astronomers saw a big storm in its atmosphere called the Great Dark Spot.

True or false?

TRUE FALSE

1. Neptune was named after a god of the mountains.

2. Uranus is the only planet to spin on its side.

3. Uranus's rings are easier to see than Saturn's.

4. Neptune has faster winds than anywhere else in the Solar System.

45

Amazing moons

All the planets from Earth to Neptune have moons.
The giant planets have dozens of them!

EUROPA

(A moon of Jupiter)
The surface is made of thick ice, and there is a hidden ocean below. There is more water in Europa's ocean than in all of Earth's water put together!

GANYMEDE

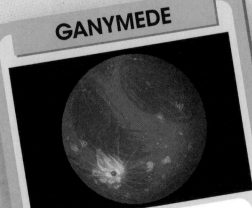

(A moon of Jupiter)
This is the largest moon in the Solar System. It is even larger than the planet Mercury.

IAPETUS

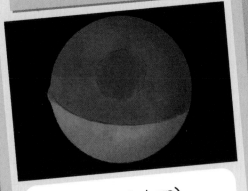

(A moon of Saturn)
This moon has two very different sides: the dark side is covered in soot, and the bright side is coated in ice.

TITAN

No swimm
in there

(A moon of Saturn)
Saturn's largest moon has lakes and rivers on its surface, but instead of water they contain a liquid similar to gasoline!

MIMAS

(A moon of Saturn)
This little moon has the largest crater in the Solar System, relative to its size. The crater is one third as wide as the moon!

MIRANDA

(A moon of Uranus)
This little moon looks all jumbled up. Some astronomers think that it may have broken into pieces that then came back together again.

 Each moon is so different! Draw and design your own here. Will it have craters? Volcanoes? What else?

IO

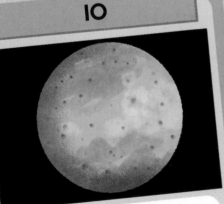

(A moon of Jupiter)
This moon has the most volcanoes in the Solar System. The volcanoes are so powerful that the lava is fired into space!

Pluto and Charon

Beyond Neptune, many smaller objects orbit the Sun, including the dwarf planet Pluto and its giant moon Charon.

Pluto

Pluto was discovered in 1930. At first astronomers thought it was a ninth planet, but we now know it is only about half the size of Earth's Moon.

Pluto takes 248 years to go around the Sun.

In 2006, it was decided that Pluto was a dwarf planet.

Moons

Pluto has five known moons. Charon, the largest, is about half the size of Pluto.

Pluto's winter lasts for hundreds of years. It gets so cold that the atmosphere around Pluto freezes solid.

Pluto and Charon are very close. They always have the same sides facing each other.

Charon

Pluto

2015, a
spacecraft
captured the
most detailed
photos of Pluto,
including an
area people call
Pluto's "heart"!

Pluto was discovered by an astronomer looking at photographs of the stars who saw that one faint "star" was in different places in different photos—meaning it was orbiting the Sun. This was no star at all. It was Pluto! Spot the difference between these two pictures to discover Pluto for yourself.

Hint: All the stars stay in the same place—Pluto is the only thing that moves!

arf planets

Solar System there is a ring
of icy blocks, called the Kuiper
iper Belt houses Pluto, as well as
re dwarf planets.

The planets are named
after ancient Roman
and Greek gods, but
astronomers have run
out of these names.
The names of dwarf
planets come from
myths told all over the
world, from Norway to
the Pacific Ocean!

Dwarf planets
A dwarf planet
is something big
enough to form into a
ball shape, but not big
enough to push all
the other space rocks
out of its orbit. Only
planets can do that.

Earth

We know of five
dwarf planets,
but astronomers
think there must
be many more.

Kuiper Belt

Oort Cloud
Beyond the Kuiper Belt
there is an even larger
cloud of icy chunks,
called the Oort Cloud.

Size guide

Dwarf planets are all smaller than Earth's Moon. They are made of ice—not just from water, but from a lot of other frozen liquids. Some of them are known to have their own moons, too.

    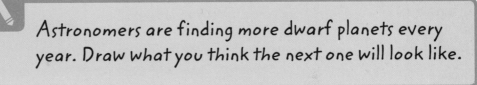

Moon   **Pluto**   **Eris**   **Haumea**   **Makemake**   **Ceres**

Astronomers are finding more dwarf planets every year. Draw what you think the next one will look like.

It's a long way back home to Earth from here!

A comet's journey

Some **comets** can appear brighter than any star in our sky. Every few years we are treated to really bright comets passing by.

> Comets are chunks of ice from the Kuiper Belt or the Oort Cloud that have fallen toward the Sun.

> They have long tails!

A comet goes through an amazing journey! Color in this comic strip to find out all about it.

1. A collision in the Kuiper Belt sends the comet toward the Sun.

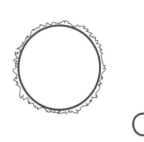

Kuiper Belt

2. To start with, the comet is a dark chunk of dirty ice that's very hard to see in space.

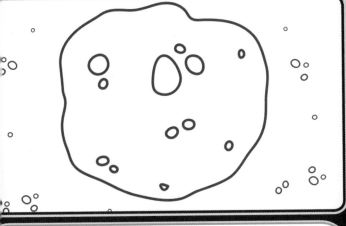

3. As it passes Jupiter, the comet begins to warm up.

Jupiter

4. People of Earth see the glowing comet and its tail. It takes a few days or weeks to fly past.

5. The comet swings around the Sun, then heads for deep space. It will be back again in a few centuries.

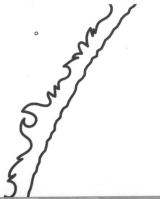

Sun

Meteor shower!

Every day, Earth's atmosphere is hit by rocks from space. But don't worry: Nearly all are no bigger than a pebble. They burn up in the sky as meteors, making streaks of light across the night sky!

When a space rock hits Earth's atmosphere, it becomes a meteor. Nearly all meteors get so hot that they burn up into gas or explode in the sky.

Meteors look like fast-moving stars to us on Earth!

We call them shooting stars, but it's really a meteor shower.

Meteorites are not like Earth's rocks. They are sometimes very heavy and contain large amounts of metal, like iron and nickel.

If the meteor is large enough, it will fall all the way to the ground. A space rock that hits the ground is called a meteorite.

Don't mix up meteors with jet planes. Meteors move about 200 times faster!

Meteor showers are when meteors are more frequent. They happen at the same time each year.

On clear nights, go outside, look up to the sky, and wait patiently.... Write down all the shooting stars you see in this chart!

Date	Time

Solar System story

Everything in the Solar System—the Sun, planets, comets, moons, and space rocks—all formed from a giant cloud of gases, ice, and dust about 4.5 billion years ago.

Here's how it all got started!

1 The giant cloud was hit by a blast coming from an exploding star far away. That caused it to spin around and start to shrink.

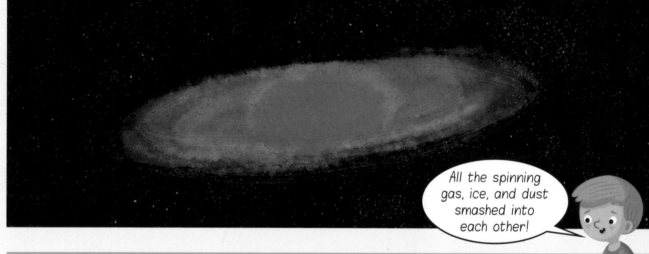

All the spinning gas, ice, and dust smashed into each other!

2 A ball of gas formed in the middle. Eventually the ball became so squashed together and hot that it became a star and started to glow.

This is our Sun!

3 After the Sun formed, there were a lot of lumps of rock and ice left over. These swirled around the Sun in a disk.

Sometimes they broke apart, and other times they stuck together.

The gravity from bigger lumps pulled smaller ones toward them.

4 By about 4 billion years ago, most of the rock, ice, and gas had collected together to make the eight planets.

And that's how we got the Solar System that we know today!

Constellations

In ancient times, people saw patterns in the sky by joining certain stars together. They named the patterns after characters from their myths and legends. These grouped stars are called **constellations**.

Orion was a great hunter. He is in a fight with Taurus the Bull.

Connect the dots to see the constellations.

5

2

3

4

6

1

7

The Big Dipper (part of the Great Bear) has been recognized since prehistoric times. Its stars are shown in cave paintings!

Ancient people could see the stars much more clearly than we can. They didn't have city lights so the sky was very dark at night.

Modern astronomers still use the ancient constellations to divide up the sky and track the stars at different times of the year.

Leo is the lion who had a fight with the hero strongman Hercules.

4

3

5

2

6

Cygnus is a swan flying across the sky. The ancient Greek god Zeus sometimes disguised himself as this bird.

What pattern do you see in these stars? Draw your own constellation and give it a name.

Seeing into space

To get a really good look at space, you need a **telescope**, and the bigger the better! A telescope collects more light than your eyes can, so it can see things in space more clearly.

Some of the biggest space telescopes are at **observatories**. Observatories are built on high mountains where the air is thin and the night sky clear.

4 The eyepiece has a lens that focuses the light into a sharp image for your eye.

3 The light beam reflects off a second mirror, which directs it into the eyepiece.

2 A large mirror at the end reflects the starlight.

The mirror is curved, so all the light forms into a smaller beam.

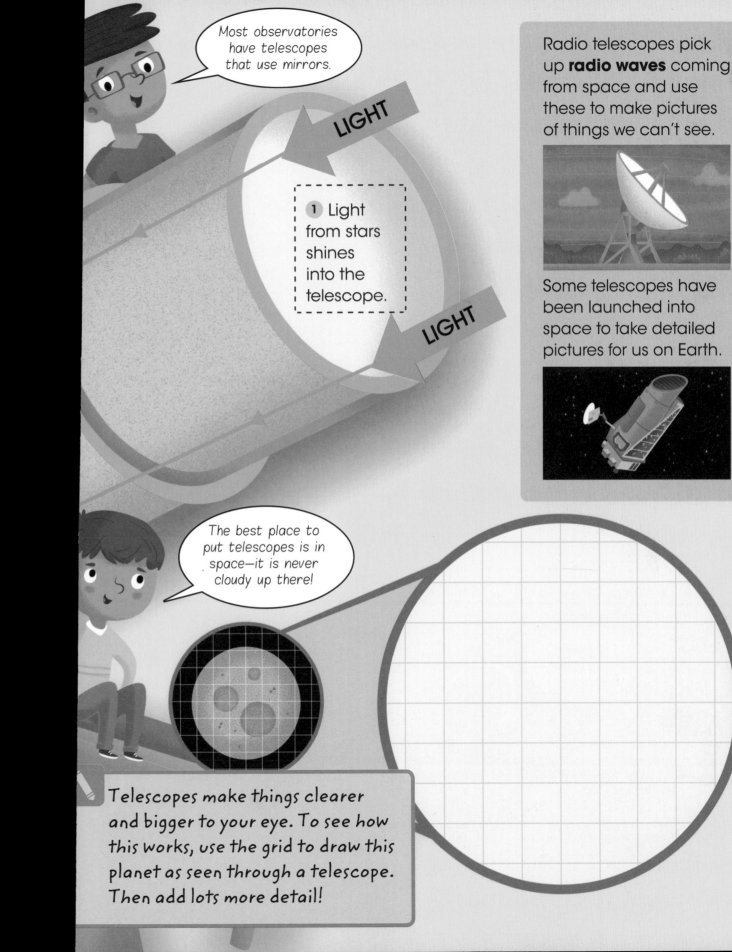

Most observatories have telescopes that use mirrors.

LIGHT

1 Light from stars shines into the telescope.

LIGHT

Radio telescopes pick up **radio waves** coming from space and use these to make pictures of things we can't see.

Some telescopes have been launched into space to take detailed pictures for us on Earth.

The best place to put telescopes is in space—it is never cloudy up there!

Telescopes make things clearer and bigger to your eye. To see how this works, use the grid to draw this planet as seen through a telescope. Then add lots more detail!

On the inside

All the light we can see in the night sky is coming from stars like our Sun—immense balls of gas that make light and heat from deep inside them.

The Sun shines its light in all directions at once.

Core
The hydrogen at the Sun's core is very hot and tightly packed together. When two hydrogen atoms are squashed together in the right way, they fuse—merging into one bigger atom and releasing a lot of light and heat energy. That process is called nuclear fusion.

Inner zone
The energy moves out of the core and travels very slowly through the middle of the huge ball of superhot gas. It takes 100,000 years to get to the outer zone!

The Sun is like a nuclear reactor!

☄ JUNIOR ASTRONOMER!

The light coming from the Sun is white, even though it contains every color you can think of. Make this color spinner to see why!

You will need:

- Construction paper
- Scissors
- Coloring pens
- A compass
- A pencil

Outer zone

Once at the outer zone, it takes about 10 days for the hot gas to rise to the surface. Then the heat and light shine out into space.

1

Use your compass to draw a circle on the paper. Cut it out.

2

Draw lines to create seven equal segments. Color them red, orange, yellow, green, blue, indigo, and violet.

3

With an adult's help, pierce the center of the circle with a pencil.

4

Spin between the palm of your hands. What color do you see?

When all the colors are mixed together, you get white!

The biggest stars!

The Sun is huge compared to our planet, and most stars are about the same size as our Sun. But there are many much bigger stars out there, too! The largest ones are huge, cool stars called **red giants**.

VY Canis Majoris
One of the largest stars ever found is VY Canis Majoris. If it were at the center of our Solar System, it would reach all the way to at least Jupiter.

Betelgeuse

Betelgeuse is pronounced "beetle juice"!

It is tricky measuring how big other stars are. Bigger stars are not always brighter than smaller ones, and even bright stars look faint when they are very far away!

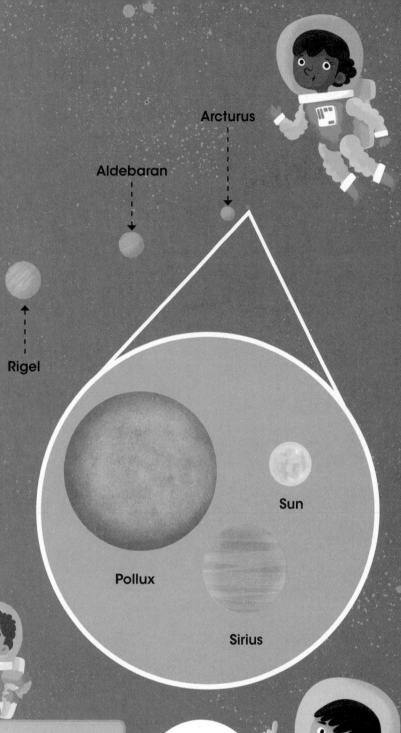

Arcturus

Aldebaran

Rigel

Sun

Pollux

Sirius

Antares

Sirius, also known as the Dog Star, is the brightest star in our sky. It is not much bigger than the Sun.

Color chart

The color of a star tells us how hot it is:

| Very hot: 54,000°F | Hot (like our Sun): 12,000°F | Fairly cool: 7,000°F | Cool: 3,500°F |

The life of a star

A star does not last forever. Eventually it runs out of the gases that fuel it and keep it shining. What happens then?

NEBULA

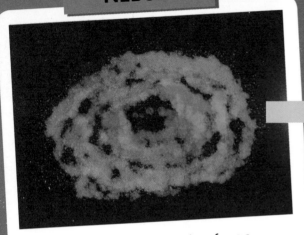

Stars are born in clouds of gas (nebulas). They then have enough energy to shine for many years.

AVERAGE STAR

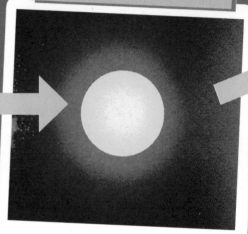

A star like the Sun has enough fuel for about 10 billion years. For most of that time, it is known as a yellow dwarf.

True or false?

		TRUE	FALSE
❶	Stars last forever.	☐	☐
❷	A white dwarf is larger than a red giant.	☐	☐
❸	A red giant is hotter than the Sun.	☐	☐
❹	The Sun will one day become a white dwarf star.	☐	☐

RED GIANT

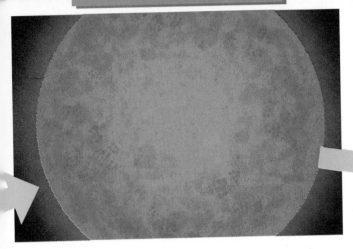

Near the end of its life, the star runs out of hydrogen. It starts fusing other gases, like helium, to make its heat and light. That makes the star swell up 100 times! This kind of star is called a red giant.

NEBULA

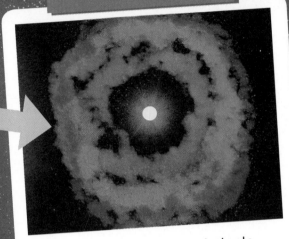

Eventually, the red giant starts shrinking. It throws out clouds of gas and dust, forming a cloud. This sometimes looks like a planet, so it is called a planetary nebula.

It is called "red" because it is not very hot and the glow becomes reddish orange.

WHITE DWARF

In the middle of the nebula is what is left of the old star's core. It is the last time we see the star shining. This is called a white dwarf.

Eventually the white dwarf cools down and stops shining.

67

Black holes

The biggest stars do not just fade away like dwarf stars. When they run out of fuel they produce the biggest bangs in the universe. What is left behind is very strange indeed...

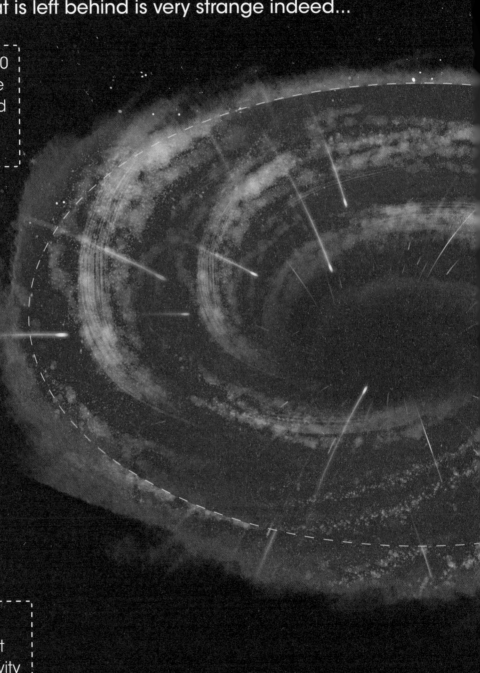

If a star is more than 20 times heavier than the Sun, it will explode and its core will collapse to form a black hole.

1 When the star runs out of fuel, it explodes in a supernova.

2 During a supernova the star's core is crushed so much that it shrinks down to the size of a pinhead. Or even smaller!

3 The tiny object is called a black hole. It has super-strong gravity that sucks everything toward it—even light!

Careful, stay back! Anything that crosses this line will be sucked into the black hole... and will never get out again.

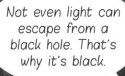

Not even light can escape from a black hole. That's why it's black.

Not all supernovas make black holes. Some produce neutron stars, which are about the size of a big city. A sugar-cube sized piece of a neutron star weighs more than Mount Everest!

Amazing Facts!

- For just a few weeks, a supernova is 5 billion times brighter than the Sun.

- There is a black hole in the middle of the Milky Way that weighs more than 4 million Suns.

- Some neutron stars are very powerful magnets. If one sat next to our Moon, its magnetism would stop computers on Earth from working!

Galaxies

Some of the lights in the night sky aren't stars—they're distant clusters of billions of stars, called galaxies.

Galaxies come in different shapes. Many of them are spirals—like the Milky Way and Andromeda—but they can also be ovals, disks, or just weird cloud shapes.

The nearest big galaxy to the Milky Way is called Andromeda. It is not that near, though—the light from Andromeda takes 2.5 million years to travel all the way to Earth!

Astronomers think most galaxies have a black hole in the middle.

Big spiral galaxies often have a thick bar of stars in the center.

That looks like our galaxy – the Milky Way!

Spiral galaxies have arms curling outward around a bulge of stars in the center.

Disk-shaped galaxies are old spiral galaxies. The arms have all merged together.

Spherical (ball-shaped) galaxies are the largest and oldest of all. They are formed when galaxies crash into each other.

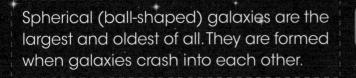

Become a galaxy spotter. What kind of galaxies are these? Spiral, spherical, disk, or cloudlike?

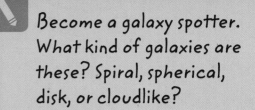

The Milky Way and Andromeda will form into an oval galaxy in 4 billion years!

Small, cloudlike galaxies are pulled into strange shapes by the pull of gravity from bigger galaxies nearby.

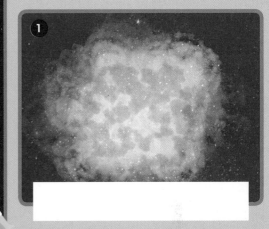

1

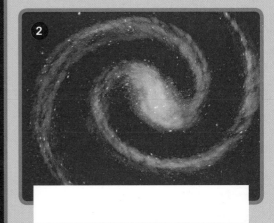

2

3

Rocket power

To get into space, astronauts blast off in a capsule on top a rocket. What lifts them into space is a controlled explosion of heat and fire!

This is real-life rocket science!

Fuel

Pumps and valves

Fuel is mixed with oxygen at the bottom of the rocket, and—boom— catches fire!

JUNIOR ASTRONOMER!

Make your own rocket with everyday items!

You will need:

- A balloon
- String
- A straw
- 2 chairs

Warning! Children can choke or suffocate on uninflated or broken balloons. Adult supervision required. Keep uninflated balloons away from children and discard broken balloons at once.

1 Thread the string through the straw.

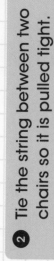

2 Tie the string between two chairs so it is pulled tight.

③ Blow up the balloon, but do not tie off the end. Carefully tape the balloon to the straw (you might need some help!).

④ Pull the balloon to one end of the string and let go!

> The balloon flies along the string because it is working like a rocket. As the balloon pushes the air out the back, the air pushes the balloon forward!

The hot gases and flames blast out of a nozzle at the base of the rocket. The force of the blast in one direction pushes the rocket in the opposite direction, then it moves faster and faster.

Combustion chamber

Reaction

Action and reaction

Rockets work by a system of **forces** called action and reaction. The action force comes from the burning fuel that pushes the hot gases and flames backward. Every action force has a reaction force. The reaction is a force that pushes the rocket forward.

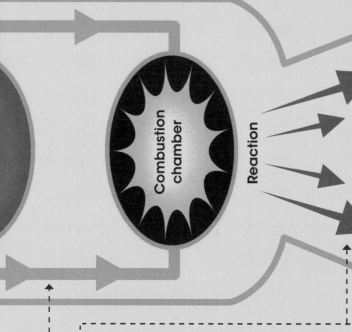

> The same thing happens when you step off a boat.

> As you push yourself forward to step off the boat, the boat will move backward.

In orbit

Once it reaches space, a spacecraft can go into orbit. If it is moving fast enough, it will circle around Earth over and over again.

An orbiting spacecraft is held in place by Earth's gravity. That stops it flying off into deep space. But what stops it falling back down to the surface?

ORBIT EXPLAINED

A

When you hit a tennis ball, it goes up and sideways. Then it keeps moving sideways, but at the same time gravity pulls it down to Earth.

B

The ball goes in a big curve.

When a space rocket flies into space, it goes in a curve as well. It is traveling very fast so it gets much higher than the tennis ball, but Earth's gravity is still pulling on it.

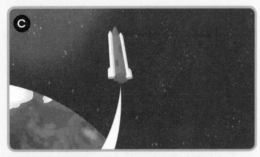

C

If the rocket travels at just the right speed, gravity stops it from flying in a straight line into deep space. Instead, the rocket curves around the world.

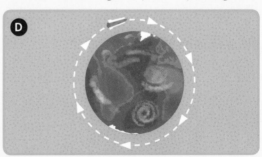

D

When the speed is just right, the spacecraft will curve all the way around the planet and end up back where it started.

JUNIOR ASTRONOMER!

See for yourself how a spacecraft stays in orbit, using a ball and a bag.

You will need:
- A ball
- A thick shopping bag
- String

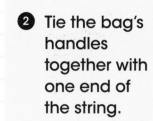

1 Put the ball in the shopping bag.

2 Tie the bag's handles together with one end of the string.

3 Go outside. With plenty of room, hold onto the other end of the string and swing the ball and bag around.

The ball is like the spacecraft, and the string is like the force of gravity. The ball would move in a straight line if the string did not keep pulling it back. So the ball just goes around and around—in an orbit!

Most of the spacecraft in orbit are satellites. They do not have any crew members on board. Satellites are automatic machines that do different jobs in space.

GPS

The satellites that tell a car's navigation system where it is orbit about 12,000 miles up. There are 32 GPS satellites spread around the world.

Communication

Satellites that send television pictures and other communications orbit around 22,000 miles above us, at the same speed that Earth rotates. That means they are always above the same part of Earth, day and night.

Spy

Spy satellites have powerful cameras that can spot houses, cars, and even people all the way from space. They orbit over the North and South Poles and scan the whole surface of Earth as they fly overhead.

Radar

Some radar satellites orbit as close as 500 miles up from the Earth. They are used to observe oceans, sea ice, land, plants, and more.

Famous rockets

About 7,000 spacecraft have been launched into space using rocket power. Here are some of the most famous rockets in history.

The Saturn V is still the most powerful rocket ever built.

Fireworks
When: At least 800 years ago
Where: China
What: The first rockets were fireworks powered by exploding gunpowder. The fireworks were used as weapons, as well as in colorful displays.

Saturn V
When: 1960s
Where: USA
What: The largest rocket ever made was built to carry astronauts to the Moon. It was over 350 feet tall—taller than the Statue of Liberty!

Space Shuttle
When: 1980s–2000
Where: USA
What: The space shuttles were half rocket, half glider. They were built to blast into space like a rocket and fly home again like a glider.

boosting
y rocket
nowledge!

Ariane 5
When: 1996–now
Where: Europe
What: This rocket's solid propellant boosters are the largest ever produced in Europe. They are attached to the side of the rocket.

Falcon 9
When: Now
Where: USA
What: This rocket takes satellites and spacecraft into orbit. Scientists are working on making the bottom section able to fly back down and land, so it can be used again.

Space shuttles

Do you want to go to space? For many years the best way to get there was a special space plane, called a space shuttle. Let's take a ride in one.

❶ Liftoff!
The shuttle is launched attached to a giant fuel tank, which feeds its engines all the way to space. It gets help from two big rocket boosters.

❷ Drop away
First the boosters, then the fuel tank, fall off when they are empty.

❸ In orbit
The shuttle orbits upside down, with its top facing Earth. The crew opens the cargo bay doors and unloads what is inside.

I wonder what they'll learn this time!

Some space shuttles had laboratories so the shuttles could be used for experiments as well as for transportation.

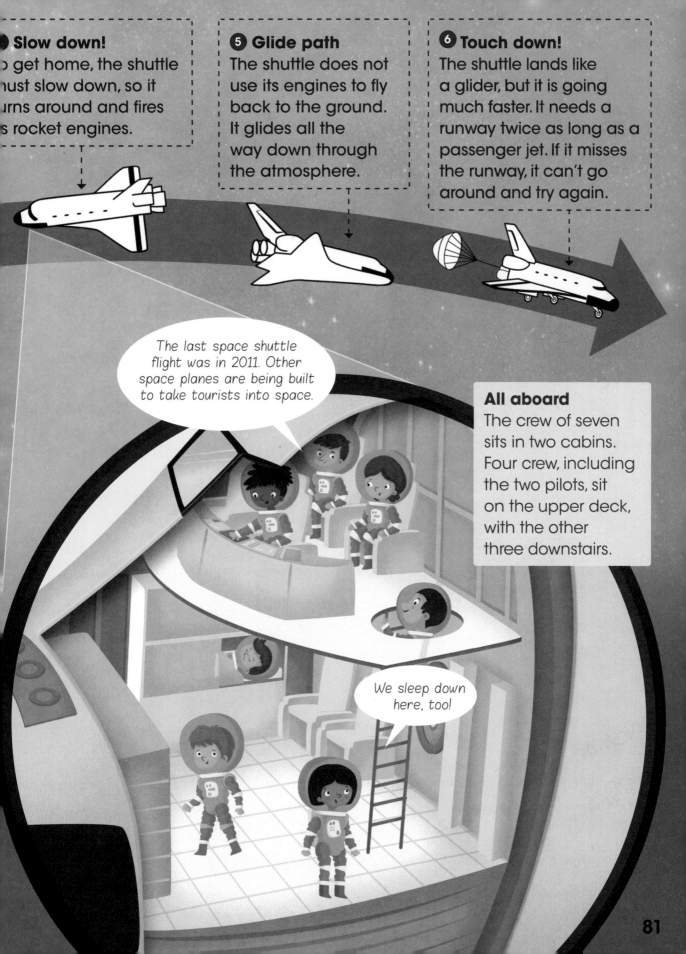

Slow down!
o get home, the shuttle
ust slow down, so it
urns around and fires
s rocket engines.

5 Glide path
The shuttle does not
use its engines to fly
back to the ground.
It glides all the
way down through
the atmosphere.

6 Touch down!
The shuttle lands like
a glider, but it is going
much faster. It needs a
runway twice as long as a
passenger jet. If it misses
the runway, it can't go
around and try again.

The last space shuttle
flight was in 2011. Other
space planes are being built
to take tourists into space.

All aboard
The crew of seven
sits in two cabins.
Four crew, including
the two pilots, sit
on the upper deck,
with the other
three downstairs.

We sleep down
here, too!

Space adventurers

Only about **500** people have ever gone to space. Here are some of the most famous space travelers.

Alexey Leonov (1965)

Another Russian cosmonau[t] this man was the first perso[n] to make a **spacewalk**. He floated by himself in space for 12 minutes!

Laika (1957)

This Russian dog was the first living thing to orbit the Earth, paving the way for people to visit space.

Yuri Gagarin (1961)

This Russian pilot was the first person to fly in space. His journey took 108 minutes and he went around the world once.

"Cosmo" means "universe," "astro" means "stars," and "-naut" means "sailor"!

Neil Armstrong (1969)

Probably the most famous spaceman of all—he was the first person to walk on the Moon!

Apollo 8 crew (1968)

Three American astronauts were the first people to fly away from Earth. They traveled to the Moon and flew around it 10 times.

Every space mission has its own badge. Design one for your own space mission!

The badge shows what we will do in space. What is our mission this time?

Liftoff!

Stand by for liftoff! The rocket is on the launchpad and the countdown has begun. 10, 9, 8, 7, 6...

The video link above shows the rocket crew during the flight. Draw your expression as you lift off!

Tower
A launch tower holds the rocket upright as it is pumped full of fuel. At the last minute, the tower lets go.

← Stage 3

← Stage 2

← Stage 1

This rocket has three stages. Each stage has its own supply of fuel and works by itself.

The crew sits in this cone at the top. There is not much room, and they are strapped tightly into their seats.

Stage 1 is the biggest section at the bottom. It is used to lift the rocket off the ground and high into the sky.

That stage then falls off, and stage 2 takes over.

Stage 3 is used to power the rocket

85

All aboard!

We've made it into orbit. Let's take a look around the spacecraft.

We go to the toilet in the spacecraft, too!

The crew sits in the middle cabin during takeoff and landing. Only this cabin parachutes back to Earth.

This cabin carries equipment and food.

Hatch
This is a door at the front for going on spacewalks or moving to other spacecraft.

1

2

Antenna
A radio dish used to communicate with mission control.

Are you a spacecraft expert? Label the diagram with the correct letter to show which bit of the spacecraft does what. Then color it all in!

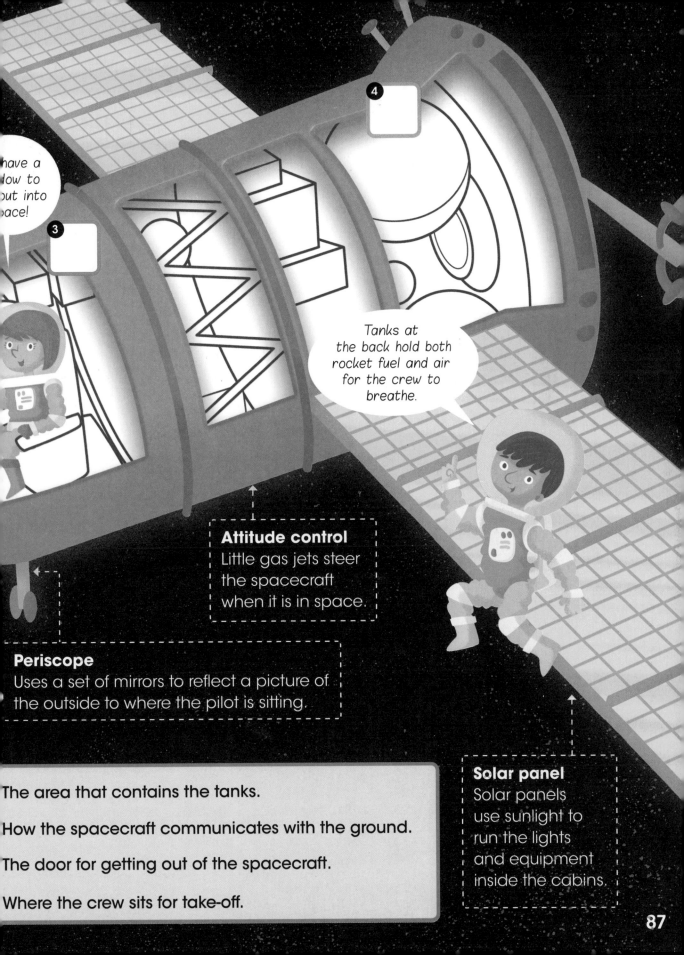

Feeling weightless

Astronauts float around their spacecraft—they are weightless! This is because the people and everything else inside the spacecraft are moving around Earth at exactly the same speed.

There is no up or down when you are weightless. Whichever way you are facing feels the same.

Being weightless means your muscles do not have much to do. After a long time in space, the muscles begin to get weak.

We have to exercise for hours every day to stay healthy!

JUNIOR ASTRONOMER!

See weightlessness in action with a simple cup and water!

You will need:

● A polystyrene cup ● A pencil ● Water

1 Ask an adult to help you carefully poke two holes on opposite sides at the bottom of the cup.

2 Over a sink, fill the cup with water. The water will start pouring out of the holes.

3 Drop the cup into a bathtub and watch carefully while it falls. What happens?

You should see that the water stops coming out of the cup as the cup falls. The water and the cup are falling at the same time—so instead of falling out because of gravity, the water moves with the cup. Like being weightless!

Suited up

Sun

There is no air in space. When astronauts go outside the spacecraft, they have to wear a space suit to stay alive.

The space suit needs to keep the astronaut both warm and cool.

In the sun, space is hotter than boiling water!

You can't see my face through the helmet.

The helmet has a bright light and camera.

A gold visor blocks out the bright sunlight.

The top half of the suit is hard, like armor.

The astronaut controls the suit using buttons on the chest.

The suit is airtight and blown up like a balloon.

The oxygen tank and suit batteries are on the back.

The arms and legs are flexible tubes of material.

Staying in touch

Spacecraft communicate with mission control using radio signals. There is a big network of radio receivers, transmitters, and ground stations all around the world.

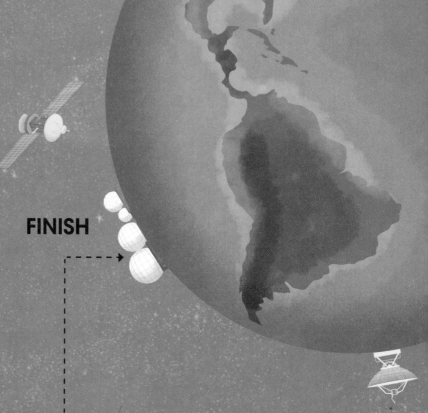

A dish is a really huge radio antenna. It is shaped like this so it can pick up very faint radio signals coming from space.

Once a dish picks up a signal from the spacecraft passing overhead, it needs to send that signal all the way back to mission control.

FINISH

Mission control could be on the other side of the world. The message is bounced from dish to communication satellite to dish, until it gets to the headquarters.

Communication satellites pick up signals from the dish and pass them on.

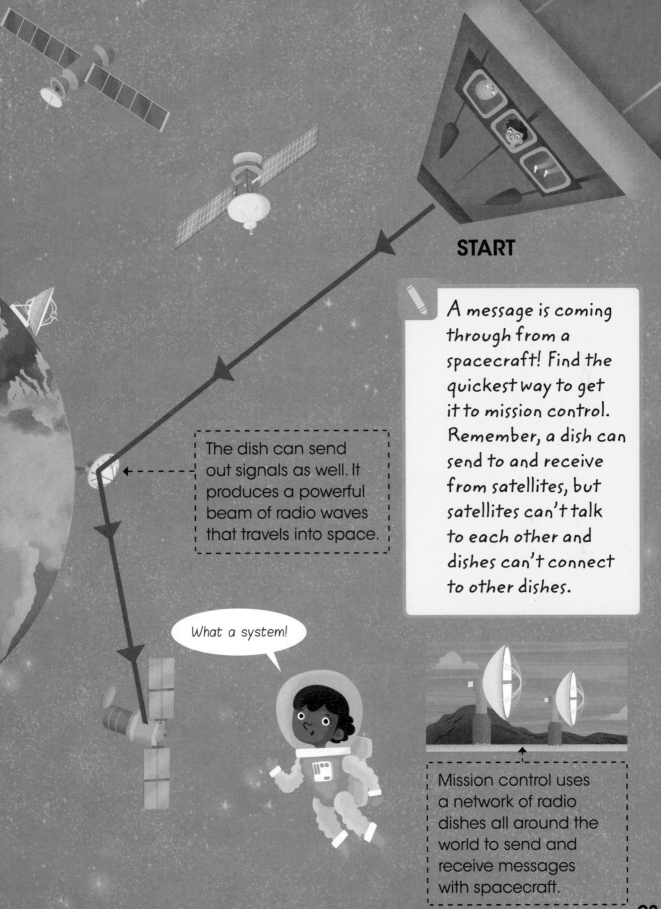

START

A message is coming through from a spacecraft! Find the quickest way to get it to mission control. Remember, a dish can send to and receive from satellites, but satellites can't talk to each other and dishes can't connect to other dishes.

The dish can send out signals as well. It produces a powerful beam of radio waves that travels into space.

What a system!

Mission control uses a network of radio dishes all around the world to send and receive messages with spacecraft.

Getting home

To head home, a spacecraft uses rocket engines to slow down for reentry. After that, gravity does the rest and the space travelers just fall back down to the ground!

This module is ready to land! It can either "splashdown" in the sea or land in a flat, empty area like the desert. Find a way through the clouds to a safe landing site. Avoid mountains or crowded cities!

There is a heat shield on the front that stops the spacecraft burning up.

1 To leave orbit, the spacecraft needs to slow down. It does this by firing its rocket one last time.

2 The fuel tanks, engine, and other parts of the spacecraft drop off. Only the crew cabin, or **module**, will travel back to earth.

3 The module falls into the atmosphere at a very high speed. That makes it very hot, just like a shooting star.

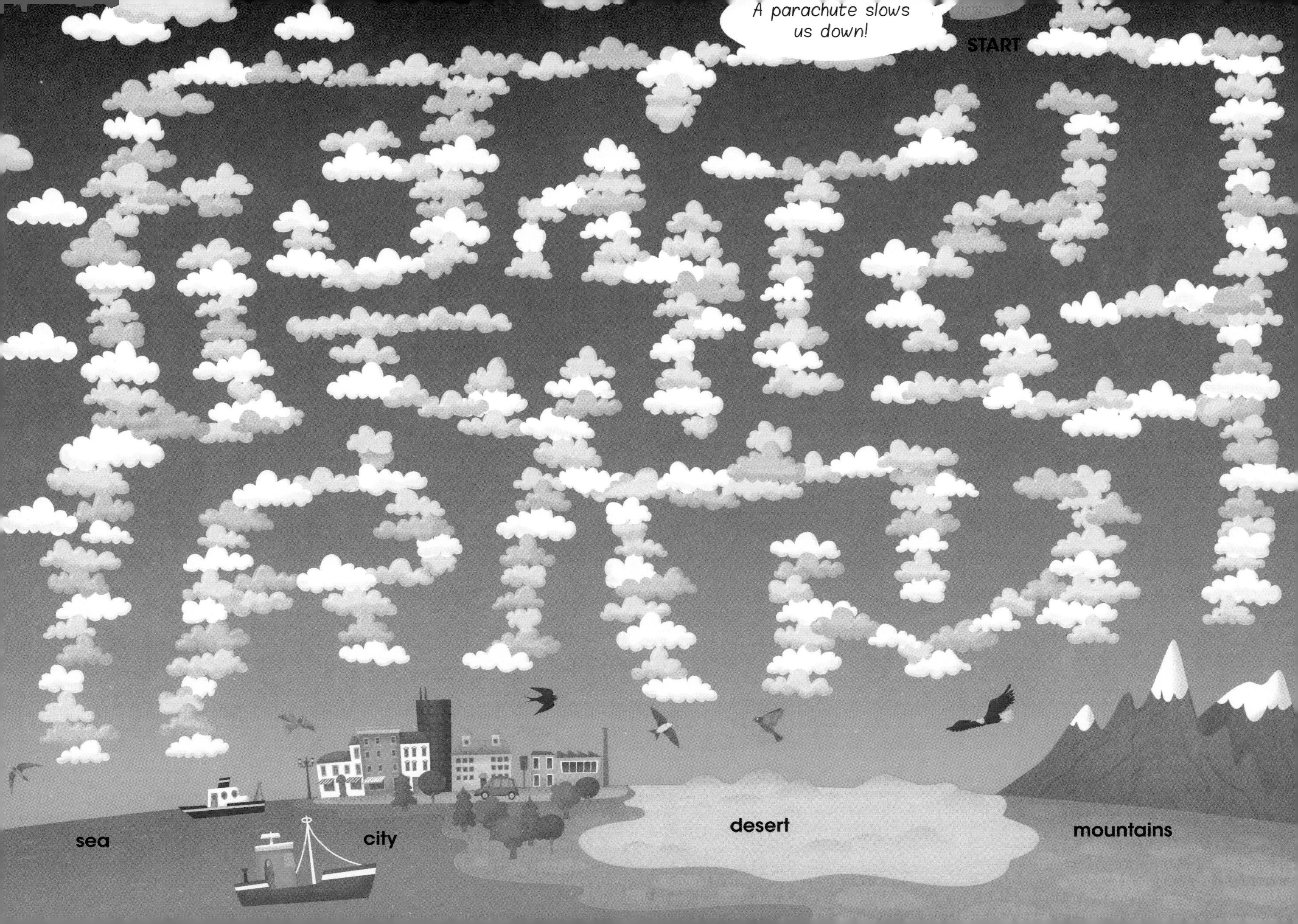
A parachute slows us down!
START
sea
city
desert
mountains

To the Moon

The Apollo missions took astronauts to orbit and land on the Moon. The Moon is the only object in space that people have visited.

Lunar means "of the moon."

2 ORBITS EARTH

1 LIFTOFF!

3 REDIRECTS TO THE MOON

There have been six successful missions to land on the Moon. Each time, there was a crew of three astronauts.

The world's biggest rocket, the Saturn V, launched the astronauts into space, pushing them away from Earth toward the Moon.

The spacecraft was made up of two parts: the orbiter and lander.

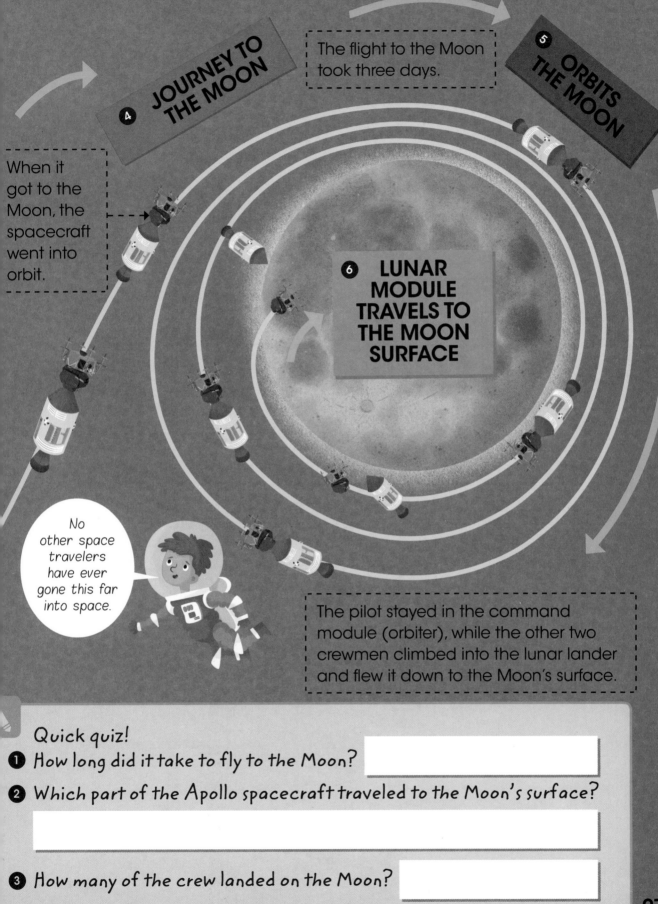

JOURNEY TO THE MOON ④

The flight to the Moon took three days.

⑤ **ORBITS THE MOON**

When it got to the Moon, the spacecraft went into orbit.

⑥ **LUNAR MODULE TRAVELS TO THE MOON SURFACE**

No other space travelers have ever gone this far into space.

The pilot stayed in the command module (orbiter), while the other two crewmen climbed into the lunar lander and flew it down to the Moon's surface.

Quick quiz!
① How long did it take to fly to the Moon?
② Which part of the Apollo spacecraft traveled to the Moon's surface?

③ How many of the crew landed on the Moon?

Apollo spacecraft

The Apollo spacecraft were designed to take people to the Moon—and bring them home again.

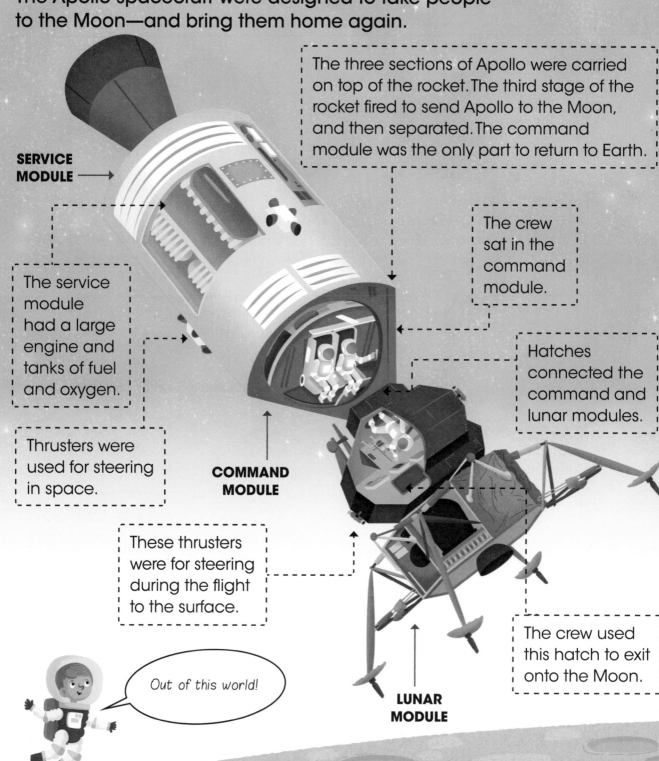

SERVICE MODULE →

The three sections of Apollo were carried on top of the rocket. The third stage of the rocket fired to send Apollo to the Moon, and then separated. The command module was the only part to return to Earth.

The crew sat in the command module.

The service module had a large engine and tanks of fuel and oxygen.

Hatches connected the command and lunar modules.

Thrusters were used for steering in space.

COMMAND MODULE

These thrusters were for steering during the flight to the surface.

The crew used this hatch to exit onto the Moon.

Out of this world!

LUNAR MODULE

JUNIOR ASTRONOMER!

 Build your own Apollo spacecraft.

You will need:
- Thick paper
- A compass
- Scissors
- A ruler
- Tape

Command module:

 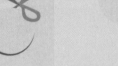 

1 Use a compass to draw a circle.

2 Cut it out.

3 Cut out a quarter of the circle. Wrap the rest into a cone. Tape and decorate.

Service module:

   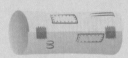

4 Use a ruler to draw a rectangle.

5 Cut it out.

6 Roll the paper into a tube. Tape and decorate.

Engine:

7 Use a compass to draw a circle.

8 Cut it out.

9 Cut out a line into the center. Wrap the rest into a cone. Tape and decorate.

Put it all together:

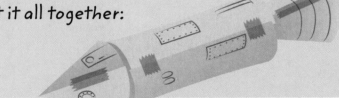

10 Tape the pieces together as shown. Your Apollo spacecraft is ready to fly!

On the Moon

Being on the Moon is very different to being on Earth. There is no sky, just the blackness of space—and you can jump really high!

The legs and landing section will be left behind.

I've left footprints everywhere!

The Apollo astronauts' moon boots left footprints in the thick dust that covers the Moon. There is no wind or rain, so these footprints will not be worn away for millions of years.

The lunar module had a small rocket that allowed the craft to land gently on the surface.

Some Moon missions brought a small, battery-powered car, or lunar rover, with them. That allowed them to explore farther from their spacecraft.

The gravity on the Moon is six times weaker than on Earth. That means everything weighs six times less than on Earth—including the astronauts!

Wheee!

The tires have no air in them. They are made of metal wires!

Moonwalking is quite hard. The astronauts found it easier to move around by making little jumps.

Astronauts left scientific equipment behind. This included a big mirror used for reflecting lasers from Earth. It allows astronomers to measure exactly how far away the Moon is.

How many footprints can you count here?

_____

A space station

The International Space Station, or ISS, is the largest spacecraft ever made. It was built in 15 countries over 12 years. There is always someone up there, every day of the year.

Robot arm
When the ISS was built, this strong mechanical arm moved parts of the space station around.

Hello again! We go around the world every hour and a half.

Science platform
Here, scientists can do experiments outside in empty space.

Cupola
This cabin has loads of windows. It gives the crew an amazing view of Earth.

Space laboratory
This science lab is used for doing experiments in weightlessness—experiments that are impossible on Earth!

Solar panels
The space station uses as much electricity as 125 houses! All that power comes from huge solar panels.

A supply ship brings food and water from Earth—and takes away the trash. Phew!

Radiators
These wavy panels let heat escape into outer space so the space station doesn't get too hot.

Crew vehicle
The crew uses a little spacecraft to get to the space station from Earth and back again. A crew of three travels at once.

True or false?

		TRUE	FALSE
1	The ISS uses the Sun to make its electricity.	☐	☐
2	The robot arm is used to pull aliens off the space station.	☐	☐
3	The space station goes around Earth every hour and a half.	☐	☐

Living in space

Some astronauts spend several weeks in space. They sleep, eat, wash, and do all the normal things you do every day—just a bit differently!

Food is packed tightly inside plastic bags or cans, so it does not leak or go rotten.

We don't drink from cups in space. We suck water out of bags using a tube.

Washing
There is no shower or bathtub in a spacecraft. The water would not go down the drain! Instead astronauts keep clean using damp cloths.

Eating
Space food cannot be too runny—it would spill easily. It cannot be too crunchy either—the crumbs would float around and make a mess! So astronauts usually eat gooey meals that can be eaten with a spoon.

Toilet

In weightlessness, pee and poop will not go down the toilet like on Earth. So a space toilet is a bit like a vacuum cleaner: it sucks everything down it into a tank.

Solid waste is burned up in the atmosphere and liquid urine is recycled!

 Want to eat like an astronaut? Make your own squishy space food!

You will need:

- A zip-top sandwich bag
- A spoon
- Water
- Dry chocolate pudding mix

1 Add four tablespoons of dry chocolate pudding mix to a bag.

2 Slowly add water until it turns into pudding, but stop before it gets runny.

3 Zip the bag shut, then squish it to mix the pudding.

We exercise for two hours a day!

Astronauts take dry food into space and add water like this before eating!

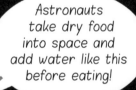

Sleeping

Sleeping in space is easy—you just float! The astronaut uses a warm, cozy sleeping bag. The bag has to be tied to the wall, ceiling, or floor of the spacecraft so it does not float away.

Working in space

Astronauts keep very busy in space. There are lots of different jobs to do to keep the station running.

Some crew members perform science experiments inside the spacecraft.

Sometimes crew members go outside to do repair work or check equipment. They wear their space suits for these spacewalks.

We're tied to the space station so we don't float away!

To get outside, I need to go through the airlock.

An airlock is a small room in the spacecraft with two doors. One leads to the main cabin, and the other out into space. Both doors are kept closed until the air pressure inside is right for an astronaut to go in or out.

Space junk

Every mission in space leaves stuff behind in orbit. There are nuts and bolts, tools, gloves, old rocket boosters, and broken satellites in space. Scientists think there are more than 21,000 pieces of space junk larger than 4 inches in orbit, and even more smaller ones.

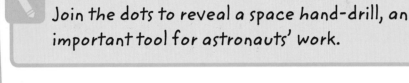

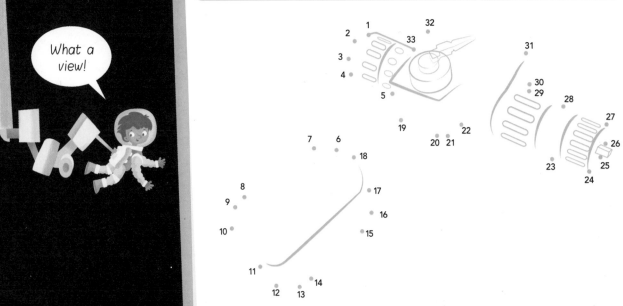

Landing on Mars

No person has ever traveled to another planet. Instead we send uncrewed landers to explore for us. The planet they visit most often is Mars.

1 A spacecraft in orbit releases a capsule that falls toward the surface of Mars. A large parachute slows down the capsule's fall.

2 A sky crane is released from the capsule.

3 The sky crane flies to the landing site. Its rockets keep it above the ground.

A parachute works only on a planet with a fairly thick atmosphere.

All we can do is watch and wait! Fingers crossed.

Gently does it! We don't want it to damage the rover.

5 The sky crane flies away from the rover and crashes in the distance.

4 The lander— this time a rover— is lowered by the sky crane onto the ground.

6 The rover has made it to Mars!

Watch the parachute help your lander land gently!

JUNIOR ASTRONOMER!

You will need:
- Thin string
- A ruler
- Scissors
- A large, thick plastic bag
- A lander, such as a clothes pin or small toy car

Make your own parachute lander!

1 Cut the string into four pieces each 6 inches long.

6 in

2 Cut a square out of the plastic bag, about 8 inches long on each side.

8 in

3 Make a little hole in each corner of the plastic and tie one piece of string to each hole.

4 Tie each string to your lander. Hold the top of the parachute in the middle and drop it carefully from somewhere high.

Warning! Plastic can be dangerous! To avoid suffocation, keep away from babies and children.

Mars rover

Several rovers have been sent to explore Mars. The biggest one so far is Curiosity. This rover is as big as a car.

Cameras take pictures of Mars.

Curiosity has six wheels. They have tough grips for rolling through sand and over rocks.

Curiosity is very slow. At top speed it can travel about 0.1 miles in one day.

A robot arm has a drill for collecting samples of rock and dust.

A laser is used to identify the chemicals in the rocks.

Rock samples are put in a tiny on-board laboratory for testing.

The rover runs on nuclear power. It will keep working for several years.

Mars is a windy place. There are thick dust storms. Curiosity cannot do its work during these storms.

The first spacecraft to successfully land on Mars was Viking 1. The lander sent back the first pictures of the red planet in 1976. People at mission control thought Mars's sky would be blue like on Earth. But they found out that its sky is actually orange most of the time because of all the red dust blowing in it!

I'm curious about Curiosity!

Rovers are looking for rocks that were formed in the presence of water, billions of years ago. Where there was water, life might have formed!

Robot explorers

Space scientists have sent dozens of probes to all parts of the Solar System. These robot explorers give us a close-up look at space.

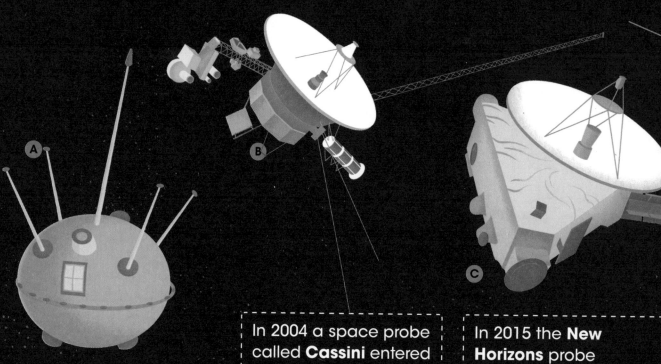

A

B

C

In 1959 **Luna 2** was the first spacecraft to reach the Moon. It crashed straight into it!

In 2004 a space probe called **Cassini** entered orbit around Saturn. It took photos and dropped a little lander called Huygens on the surface of Saturn's biggest moon, Titan.

In 2015 the **New Horizons** probe flew past the dwarf planet Pluto. It took the first close-up pictures of the surface, showing that it was covered in ices.

Pluto

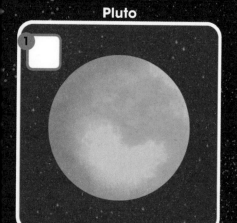

1

Saturn

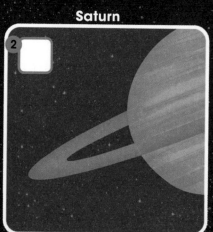

2

A comet

3

Match each satellite to its mission.

D

E

F

In 1979 and the 1980s, two space probes called Voyager flew past Jupiter, Saturn, Uranus, and Neptune. They made discoveries about the planets and their moons.

In 1990 the **Hubble** Space Telescope was launched into orbit. Hubble is the best space telescope ever built. It can see things 13 billion light-years away!

In 2014 the **Philae** lander was the first spacecraft to touch down on a comet. It tested the chemicals in the comet's ice.

Things in deep space

Jupiter, Saturn, Uranus, Neptune

The Moon

4

5

6

Looking for aliens

As far as we know, Earth is the only planet to have life on it. However, many astronomers think there is life somewhere else in the universe...

People looking for aliens use radio dishes to collect radio waves from space. They are hoping to find signals sent from another planet.

Our powerful radio and television signals go into space. One day, they might be heard by aliens looking for us!

If we do hear an alien signal, it will have been traveling through space toward us for hundreds of years—probably more.

If we ever meet aliens, what will they look like? Draw an amazing alien here.

Hello? Is anyone there?

Life on other planets would probably be tiny microbes, not large animals or people like us. But no one knows!

The Kepler telescope is searching space for planets that orbit other stars. It has found many hundreds so far. Some are even made of rock, like Earth!

To space and back

A spaceplane is a spacecraft that can travel in space and then fly down to the ground again, like an airplane. Unlike other spacecraft, spaceplanes can be used more than once.

Spaceplanes could help many more people explore the space around Earth. They might make exploration or delivery missions.

The spaceplane lands on a normal runway and then can be used over and over again.

Right, let's get it ready for the next flight.

This spaceplane has a mission to deliver cargo to the ISS. It docks with the space station to unload.

A spaceplane can take off, fly, and land using a human pilot—or without one!

Special tiles protect the spaceplane from the extreme heat of re-entering the atmosphere.

Easy does it!

Draw yourself as the pilot!

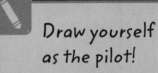

Spaceliners

One day people might be flying into space every day: space tourism! A rocket-powered passenger spacecraft could fly across the world much faster than today's airliners.

Spaceliners might use new kinds of engines called scramjets. These work like a jet engine and a rocket all at once and are super powerful.

Would you like to travel on a spaceliner one day?

Time to fly!

A spaceliner takes off straight up, like a rocket. But instead of going into orbit, it flies in a curve up and out of the atmosphere. It then travels around the world on the edge of space, before flying back down into the air. Then it lands just like a plane.

Into the future

Making spacecraft is expensive, and getting them into space takes a huge amount of fuel. In the future we will use new ways to make getting into space easier.

Launching from the air

Airplanes are better fliers than rockets. Some spacecraft can be launched from an aircraft flying very high. That means the space rocket does not need so much fuel.

Powered by light

Spacecraft use fuel to move around and change orbit, but this is expensive and heavy. To save on cost and weight, spacecraft could use pressure from the Sun. A solar sail is a huge sheet of metal foil that can catch this light.

Pack your sunglasses!

Inflatable space stations

Soon the first inflatable space station will be launched. It is made from tough but flexible plastic instead of metal. The plastic is folded into a small package for launch. Once in space it is pumped up with air to many times the size!

I've never lived inside a balloon before!

What will space travel be like in the future? Draw your own invention here.

A new world

One day people might go live on another planet or moon. They will need to take lots with them to build their new home, but they might be able to use local rocks and dust for building materials.

Let's take a look around a possible new world...

There will be a space station in orbit around the new world. This is where people will arrive when they travel from Earth.

This colony has been built on a moon where there is water deep in the rocks. The water is used for drinking, and it can also be turned into the rocket fuel the colony needs.

Out here there is nothing to breathe. We have to use spacesuits.

The spacecraft from Earth arrives with empty fuel tanks. These could be converted into buildings for the space colonists to live in.

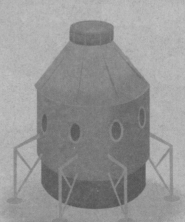

The colony needs to grow its own food inside greenhouses.

The colony keeps in touch with Earth using powerful radio transmitters.

Imagine you have moved to a space colony. What is your view from your bedroom window? Draw it here.

The air inside these greenhouses is the same as on Earth!

Electricity is made by solar panels.

The Sun is weaker here, so it's very cold... Brrr!

Small craters or caves might be good places for colonies. High walls will protect the buildings from any winds or incoming meteorites.

Glossary

Asteroid A space rock that orbits the Sun. Most are in a big band between Mars and Jupiter, known as the Asteroid Belt.

Atmosphere The layer of gases that surrounds a planet or moon. Earth's atmosphere is known as the air.

Atoms Tiny building blocks that are inside everything in the Universe—including your body!

Aurora Colorful lights that fill the sky near the North and South Poles, caused by hot gases streaming out of the Sun.

Axis The imaginary line that runs through Earth or any other object that spins around. The line shows which way the object spins.

Big Bang The start of the Universe, where everything that is now in space was packed into a small super-hot ball that has expanded ever since.

Comets Balls of ice from the edge of the Solar System that swing around the Sun, leaving a tail of dust and gas.

Constellations Patterns in the stars seen by ancient people. Most are based on animals and gods.

Expand To grow larger in all directions.

Forces The pushes and pulls that make things move.

Galaxies Huge groups of stars found across the universe.

Gas A wispy substance that spreads out and fills any container, such as air.

Gas giant A big planet made mostly of a swirly ball of gas.

Gravity The force that pulls objects together. Gravity makes thing fall to the ground and also keeps planets orbiting the Sun.

Hydrogen An invisible gas that is very lightweight and catches fire easily.

Magnet A metal object that is surrounded by a force field. Most metal things that come into the force field are pulled toward the magnet.

Meteor A small space rock that hits Earth's air and burns up in a bright shooting star.

Meteorite The rocky remains of a large meteor that make it all the way to the ground.

Minerals Natural substances found in rocks, such as sand, chalk, and coal.

Module A section of a spacecraft that can be connected to other modules. Each module has a particular job and can be detached when not needed any more.

Nebulas Vast clouds of gas in space.

Observatories The place where space scientists—astronomers—look at objects in outer space. Observatories have the world's largest telescopes.

Orbits The path that a planet takes around a star. Orbits are always ovals, or squashed circles.

Ozone A special version of oxygen gas that forms a layer high in the atmosphere.

Phases The different shapes the Moon has as it moves through the sky each month—we can only see the part that is lit up by the Sun.

Planets Objects we can see in the night sky that move around in a different way to the stars, because they are orbiting the Sun.

Radio waves Invisible waves that come from space. We also make these waves to send messages, radio broadcasts, TV shows, and phone calls.

Red giants Big stars that are not as hot as our Sun and so they glow red.

Satellite A natural or human-made object that orbits a planet.

Shepherd moons Tiny moons in Saturn's rings. Their gravity helps to keep the rocks inside the rings in place.

Solar System Our local neighborhood in space made up of the planets, moons, comets, and asteroids that move around the Sun.

Spacewalks When an astronaut leaves the spacecraft and floats around outside. Spacewalks are needed for doing repairs on spacecraft.

Stars Huge balls of gas that give out light and heat. The Sun is our nearest star.

Telescope A device designed to make distant objects appear nearer.

Universe The name for the whole of space, including all the stars, galaxies, and nebulas—and a huge amount of empty space!

Index

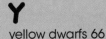

Answers

Pages 10-11
1–B, 2–C, 3–A

Page 19
1–B, 2–C, 3–A

Page 25
1–Summer, 2–Winter

Pages 28-29
There are 31 craters.

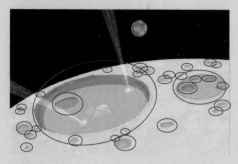

Page 35
1–False, 2–True, 3–True, 4–False

Pages 38-39

Page 41

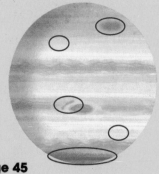

Page 45
1–False, 2–True, 3–False, 4–True

Page 49

Page 66
1–False,
2–False,
3–False,
4–True

Page 71
1–Cloudlike, 2–Spiral, 3–Disk

Page 77
1–Spy, 2–Radar, 3–GPS, 4–Communication

Pages 86-87
1–C, 2–B, 3–D, 4–A

Pages 92-93

Page 95

Pages 100-101
There are 15 footprints.

Page 103
1–True, 2–False, 3–True

Page 97
1–It took three days to travel to the Moon, 2–The lunar lander traveled to the Moon's surface, 3–Two of the crew landed on the Moon.

Pages 112-113
1–C, 2–B, 3–F, 4–E, 5–D, 6–A